Biblical Christianity is Evangelical

(Not Political)

Book #1 in the Little Book Series

Kent Philpott

EVP

Biblical Christianity is Evangelical

All rights reserved.
Earthen Vessel Media, LLC
San Rafael, CA 94903
www.evpbooks.com

ISBN: 978-1-946794-06-2

Library of Congress Control Number: 2018947535

Cover and interior design by KLC Philpott

Acknowledgment

Prior to and throughout the writing of this "Little Book," I have enjoyed the inspiration and encouragement of my dear friend John Konieczko, who lives in Columbia, South Carolina.

John, converted during the Jesus People Movement, and I are of one mind and heart, that is to continue as we did so many years ago to boldly proclaim the message of our Lord Jesus.

At the beginning of this project, while John was visiting Katie and me in Marin County, we began talking about the content of this present volume. I told him, "John, this will be our book together."

And it is. Thank you John.

Kent Philpott
April 25, 2018
San Rafael, CA

Contents

Preface

Evangelical means different things to different people, and in more recent times it has acquired a negative and political bite, yet just decades ago it was an honored term without political connotations. No more. In the present climate, evangelicals have been reduced to a block of voters who are viewed as extreme right wing or even narrow-minded bigots.

The purpose of this little book is to show the biblical understanding of *evangelical* and describe what a biblical evangelical is. My intention is to show that, from a biblical point of view, the bold proclamation of the essential and core message of Christianity, otherwise known as the gospel, is what accurately defines an evangelical.

Not all the visible church is evangelical. Likely only a small fraction of this public, organized, and Christian-oriented designation is the actual Church *known by God*. This Church, referred to as the *invisible* Church, is made up of all those who are born from above, forgiven of sin, indwelt by the Holy Spirit, and placed into the Body of Christ. It consists of persons in many different backgrounds, races, ethnicities, nationalities, and organizations. Denominationally, some are Roman Catholic, Baptist, Eastern Orthodox, Pentecostal, and independents. Indeed, born-from-above people will be found among the more than 30,000 organized denominations. Then, there are complete loners who do not identify with any gathering of Christians.

Within many of the organized groupings of Christians, even those who have a *sacramental*[1] theology, are those who engage in bold proclamation of the person and work of Jesus Christ.[2] However, sacramentalism often leans heavily on the ministrations of the church, resulting in either a "light" approach to the gospel or an ignoring of it all together.

Biblical evangelicalism has appeared a number of times in Christian history, including during the great Reformation of the sixteenth century. Many countries have also experienced *awakenings*, sometimes called revivals, of which America has experienced four: those of 1734–1742, then 1798–1825, 1857–

---

1   Sacramental means those who identify with churches that believe that the church itself, through the rituals of its ministers, convey salvation and usually by means of church membership, baptism, and receiving of the Lord's Supper, or communion, or the mass.

2   *Person* refers to who Jesus is, God in the flesh, God with us, fully God and fully man. *Work* means that which has to do with what Jesus did in His dying on the cross, His burial, His resurrection, His ascension, and at some unknown point, His return as King of glory.

6

1859, and more recently from 1967 to 1975.

These awakenings wielded great spiritual impact but inevitably ended, and normal times drifted back in. Predictably, the church languished and declined, especially in the visible Church. This is presently the case in America—a decline across the board.

The reason for this presentation then becomes clear. This is not a call to awakening; such is only possible by the working of the Holy Spirit who alone can bring genuine awakening and revival. This "Little Book" is a call for Christians to engage in bold proclamation of the gospel of Jesus Christ.

Reader, please read slowly through the Book of Acts and discover once again its emphasis on the presentation of the core gospel message. Also read the Gospels and see what Jesus commanded His followers—us—to do until He returns at the end of the age.

This is also an invitation to join with countless others who share the core message of this book. Many who came to Christ in the Jesus People Movement of 1967 to 1975 will agree with the essential point that boldly presenting the message of Jesus is what we are called to do.

Could it be that some who read this would like to align with and be in fellowship with others who share this concept? If so, you are invited to be part of the Bold Proclamation Association. While not a clever name, it makes the point clear. This "association" has no formal membership, and no money changes hands; it is simply a fellowship of like-minded followers of Jesus.

If so, please contact: kentphilpott@comcast.net.

Chapter One

Christianity's Essential Message

The focus of this book is the bold proclamation of the Good News of Jesus Christ. Below is a history of how the gospel message came to us in the first place.

The Message

Genesis 3:15, often referred to as the proto-evangel, is the first mention in Scripture of the undoing and defeat of the enemy of God, and at once prepares the reader for a future event that will be revealed at some unknown time.

> "I will put enmity between you and the woman, and between your offspring and her offspring; he shall bruise your head, and you shall bruise his heel."

Within this oldest stratum of literature of the Hebrew Bible is the promise that the serpent will not triumph despite the expulsion of Adam and Eve from the presence of their Creator. A "woman" is introduced in Genesis 3:15, as is the offspring of that woman. After centuries of biblical history, this woman is finally revealed as the virgin of Isaiah 7:14, who gives birth to one who is "God with us"—Immanuel. It is Immanuel, according to Genesis 3:15, who will deal a deathblow to the serpent and the serpent's offspring. The Apostle John put it this way: "The reason the Son of God appeared was to destroy the works of the devil" (1 John 3:18).

Abraham, in a direct line from Adam, was elected by God to be the head of a family of people to be called Israel. Israel would cradle the Messiah, the Christ, through whom the enemy would be destroyed. The prophets of Israel made it clear that the Messiah would also be a "light to the nations" or Gentiles. (See Isaiah 11:10; 42:6; 60:3; 66:19; Joel 3:9; Micah 5:8; and Malachi 1:11, among many others.)

The "bruise your head" of Genesis 3:15 took place when Jesus of Nazareth—God in the flesh, God in person—died on a cross, bearing our sin, then rose from the dead and is now seated at the right hand of the Father. From there He will return to judge the living and the dead.

This is the essential and unchanging message that God Himself has communicated to us, which is reflected in the Apostles' Creed. The Old Roman Symbol from the second century was expanded into this wonderful statement of faith:

I believe in God, the Father almighty,
Creator of heaven and earth.
I believe in Jesus Christ, God's only Son, our Lord,
who was conceived by the Holy Spirit,
born of the Virgin Mary,
suffered under Pontius Pilate,
was crucified, died, and was buried;
He descended to the dead.
On the third day he rose again;
he ascended into heaven
and is seated at the right hand of the Father;
He will come again to judge the living and the dead.
I believe in the Holy Spirit,
the holy Catholic Church,
the communion of saints,
the forgiveness of sins,
the resurrection of the body,
and the life everlasting. Amen.

We are at the point in history where the last statement concerning Jesus Christ is most relevant: "He will come again to judge the living and the dead."

A simple way to state the core message is *Law + Grace = Gospel*. The "Law" is designed to show us that we are lawbreakers (sinners). The command to love God with our whole self makes it clear that we do not. The command to love our neighbor as ourselves further reveals our dilemma. We break

God's laws regularly, but God is utterly holy, and no sin can come before Him. This puts us in an impossible situation. If our transgressing of the law (sin) is not solved or dealt with in some way, then we must spend eternity apart from God's presence.

Since the consequence of sin is eternal death in what the Bible refers to as hell, it is understandable that this message is often ignored or softened. That law-breaking means eternal separation from God is not a welcome message, and all Christians know this. We do not want to offend, and we do not want to be rejected and ridiculed. If we are honest, we will confess that we have often conveniently proclaimed only a part of the equation—grace. Yet, law and the consequence for breaking it is an essential part of the message, so the dumbing down of that message is far less than full disclosure. The messenger has a duty to tell the whole truth.

Grace is indeed the second part of the equation. Grace—or mercy—is at the heart of Christianity, because God provides that our sin is forgiven on the basis of what God the Son did on the cross. All our sin, not in part but the whole, was laid on the Lamb of God while He hung on the cross. As far as the east is from the west, so far has our sin been removed from us, utterly forgiven and forgotten by our holy God.

Grace is a gift, freely given, and is not the result of our doing good, being devoted to religious ritual, or committing to the dictates of an organized religious institution. All the faith systems of the world, except biblical Christianity, teach in one way or another that conformity to its rules and regulations earns favor with the deity. Enlightenment, achieving God-consciousness, gaining union with the divine, absorption into the godhead, or whatever other goal the gurus promote is only another form of *works*. It is not gospel grace and leaves the practitioner empty and frustrated.

Law plus grace equals gospel: this is the message. This alone is biblical Christianity. Anything else is both a distortion and misrepresentation of what God has revealed in Scripture. There is no other true message of salvation.

From earliest times religions and doctrines have come into being that are purported to be the way to God. This is understandable, since our Creator God has put into our core being that we should seek after Him. The Apostle Paul, in his address to the Athenians at the Areopagus, said it this way:

> The God who made the world and everything in it, being Lord of heaven and earth, does not live in temples made by men, nor is he served by human hands, as though he

needed anything, since he himself gives to all mankind life and breath and everything . **. . that they should seek God, in the hope that they might feel their way toward him and find him.** (Acts 17: 24-25, 27)

By His grace alone we know that Jesus Christ is the way, the truth, and the life, and no one comes to the Father except by and through Him. This is our message.

In the next chapter we take a close look at the mission of the early church.

Chapter Two

Christianity's Essential Mission

Let us turn now to the Book of Acts and briefly note those places where we find bold proclamation of the gospel. Luke gives us a glimpse into the Christian mission of the Church in the first century, those several decades following the ascension of Jesus to the right hand of the Father.

The Mission

Here is the mission as presented by Jesus in Matthew's Gospel:

> And Jesus came and said to them, "All authority in heaven and on earth has been given to me. Go therefore and make disciples of all nations, baptizing them in the name of the Father and of the Son and of the Holy Spirit, teaching them to observe all that I have commanded you. And behold, I am with you always, to the end of the age" (Matthew 28:18-20).

And in Luke's Gospel:

15

Then he said to them, "These are my words that I spoke to you while I was still with you, that everything written about me in the Law of Moses and the Prophets and the Psalms must be fulfilled." Then he opened their minds to understand the Scriptures, and said to them, "Thus it is written, that the Christ should suffer and on the third day rise from the dead, and that repentance for the forgiveness of sins should be proclaimed in his name to all nations, beginning from Jerusalem. You are witnesses of these things" (Luke 24:44-48).

And in John's Gospel:

Jesus said to them again, "Peace be with you. As the Father has sent me, even so I am sending you" (John 20:21).

"Send" is from the word apostle. An apostle is one who is sent. All who obey the word of Jesus to witness and proclaim the person and work of Jesus is an apostle. Apostle is not a position; it is an activity. "Missionary" is the Latin equivalent for the Greek "apostle."

Book of Acts

Now we turn to the Book of Acts and note passages

16

that speak to the bold proclamation that characterized the early Christians:

> So when they had come together, they asked him, "Lord, will you at this time restore the kingdom to Israel?" He said to them, "It is not for you to know times or seasons that the Father has fixed by his own authority. But you will receive power when the Holy Spirit has come upon you, and you will be my witnesses in Jerusalem and in all Judea and Samaria, and to the end of the earth" (Acts 1:6-8).

Here we see Jesus giving his followers the commission to preach the gospel. And we also see something else—Holy Spirit empowering.

The preacher of the Gospel will be aware that words alone will not suffice; the power of the Holy Spirit is vital, utterly necessary. We must realize we are dependent on the power of the Holy Spirit and ask God to be present with us and empower our message. Some will refer to the "baptism of the Holy Spirit" or the Holy Spirit coming upon us as we witness. This is good and biblical. Of course, the concept has been distorted by some to refer to speaking in tongues, but I see it as the Holy Spirit convicting of sin and revealing Jesus to those whom God is calling to salvation.

Paul speaks of it in Romans 10:17:

> "So faith comes from hearing, and hearing through the word of Christ."

In a way that we do not understand or control, the Holy Spirit of God does the work of saving. Our responsibility is to present the core message.

Acts 2:14a

> "But Peter, standing with the eleven, lifted up his voice and addressed them."

Peter stood up and then lifted up his voice. Luke does not tell us whether Peter was scared or nervous, but as a human being we suspect there was some emotion present. He had never preached before, and he would have no way of knowing what kind of response there might be.

He tells his listeners to repent (and in 3:19 he does the same) and be baptized in the name of Jesus, meaning to identify as a follower of Jesus while acknowledging Him as Messiah and Lord. This is bold indeed.

Acts 4:12

> "And there is salvation in no one else, for there is no other name under heaven given among men by which we must be saved."

What a radical message! Absolute truth, with no apology or equivocation. If he had left the door open for other paths to God, most would have chosen one of those. By "name" Peter meant the person of Jesus, who He is, Messiah and Savior, and what He did, taking our sin upon Himself. Certainly, none of his hearers would have understood much of what he was saying. Here is the miracle then: God's Spirit doing that which nothing or no one can do.

Who of us when first told of Jesus and His gospel understood much of it? We must rely upon the inner working of the Holy Spirit to convict of sin and reveal Jesus.

Acts 4:13

> Now when they saw the boldness of Peter and John and perceived that they were uneducated, common men, they were astonished, and recognized that they had been with Jesus.

"Recognized" probably meant that Peter and John had indeed been seen in the company with Jesus. They would still have dressed like and talked like common folk from Galilee. Yet the message and the boldness made a strong impression.

Acts 4:29

> "And now Lord, look upon their threats and grant to your servants to continue to speak your word with all boldness."

During the very early period of the Church, the followers of Jesus faced strong opposition. After Peter and John rejoined the rest of the faithful community, they entered into prayer, part of which you just read. The boldness was part of the request made to God. They were not naturally bold. They were like we are, rather timid and fearful, concerned about rejection and ridicule. So they prayed.

Acts 4:31

> "And when they had prayed, the place in which they were gathered together was shaken, and they were all filled with the Holy Spirit and continued to speak the word of God with boldness."

Notice there is no mention of speaking in tongues, or falling out, or "words" from God being heard; rather, the Holy Spirit overwhelmed their natural fear and emboldened the believers in Jesus.

Acts 5:27–33

> And when they had brought them, they

20

set them before the council. And the high priest questioned them, saying, "We strictly charged you not to teach in this name, yet here you have filled Jerusalem with your teaching, and you intend to bring this man's blood upon us." But Peter and the apostles answered, "We must obey God rather than men. The God of our fathers raised Jesus, whom you killed by hanging him on a tree. God exalted him at his right hand as Leader and Savior, to give repentance to Israel and forgiveness of sins. And we are witnesses to these things, and so is the Holy Spirit, whom God has given to those who obey him." When they heard this, they were enraged and wanted to kill them.

The whole band of apostles is now before the Sanhedrin, the ruling Council of Israel. On certain matters they had the authority to condemn and execute. And these men were the spiritual and religious leaders. But something greater counted, and the missionaries, for that is the meaning of apostle, looked to Jesus for their authority. Here is clear evidence of the power of the Holy Spirit.

Most of us are not brave and fearless. We are subject to the same social and personal pressures that affect everyone. Two things make the difference, however:

one, being saved by grace and filled with the Holy Spirit; and two, being given the command to be bold witnesses for our Lord and Savior, Jesus Christ.

Acts 9:26–27

> And when he had come to Jerusalem, he attempted to join the disciples. And they were all afraid of him, for they did not believe that he was a disciple. But Barnabas took him and brought him to the apostles and declared to them how on the road he had seen the Lord, who spoke to him, and how at Damascus, he had preached boldly in the name of Jesus.

It is interesting to read that the apostles in Jerusalem, meaning Peter, Andrew, James, and John, among the others, were fearful of Paul, formerly Saul, who had been a fierce persecutor of the early believers in Jesus. However, Barnabas, the son of encouragement, testified in defense of Paul, and the main point he made was how Paul "had preached boldly in the name of Jesus."

Above all else, the bold preaching was evidence of the genuine conversion of their former antagonist.

Acts 10:42–43

> And he commanded us to preach to the

people and to testify that he is the one appointed by God to be judge of the living and the dead. To him all the prophets bear witness that everyone who believes in him receives forgiveness of sins through his name.

These words are from Peter while he was preaching to Cornelius, and others, in Caesarea. Here was a Jew in the home of a Gentile, even a Roman centurion, who boldly presented the fact that the Messiah of the Hebrew Scriptures was Jesus of Nazareth.

Some have argued it was not much of a sermon, especially considering it was presented to a Gentile gathering; nevertheless. the subsequent verses show that the Holy Spirit fell upon that group, which led to their conversion and baptism.

Acts 14:3

So they remained for a long time, speaking boldly for the Lord who bore witness to the word of his grace, granting signs and wonders to be done by their hands.

On the first missionary journey, the missionaries Paul and Barnabas visit a synagogue. A "great number of both Jews and Greeks believed." As usual, those who were not converted stir up trouble.

It must be noted that trouble will always, or nearly always, follow the preaching of the gospel. In this case, those who believe that Jesus is the Messiah may desert synagogue worship, which is a major challenge to the rest. Trouble will likely be the result. Those who did not acknowledge Jesus as Messiah and Savior stirred up certain Gentiles "and poisoned their minds against the brothers" (v. 2).

Those proclaiming the Gospel message will often be personally attacked, rather than the message itself. And seasoned Christians are well aware that Satan is threatened by gospel presentation. He wants those he has kept in the dark to remain in the dark. Spiritual warfare is all too real.

Paul and Barnabas, now with a bunch of new believers to care for, speak boldly for the Lord. And happily, miracles attested to the authenticity of their work. In genuine awakenings, like the Jesus People Movement of the late 1960s and early 1970s, God by His Holy Spirit did give signs and wonders. This is nice, even exhilarating, when it happens, but during "normal times" we see few attending miracle acts of the Spirit.

Acts 18:26

> [Apollo] began to speak boldly in the synagogue, but when Priscilla and Aquila heard

him, they took him and explained to him the
way of God more accurately.

Apollo, though he only knew the baptism of John,
was a bold proclaimer of the gospel message to the
extent he knew it. When Priscilla and Aquila heard
about him they helped fill in the blanks of those
things concerning the way of God, probably meaning
the significance of the crucifixion, resurrection, and
ascension. The point here is the boldness of Apollo.

Acts 19:8

And he entered the synagogue and for three
months spoke boldly, reasoning and per-
suading them about the kingdom of God.

Paul, fresh on his third mission, is at Ephesus. As was
his practice (see Romans 1:16), he spoke boldly for
three months in the local synagogue. Trouble inevitably surfaced, but Paul stayed two years longer than
at any other city in his missionary work.

Trouble does not always work against the proclaimer of the gospel; in fact, it may be beneficial.
Often it is a case that "no publicity is bad publicity."
Others may wonder what the fuss is all about and, as
a result, hear the gospel proclaimed. Boldness works
wonders sometimes.

The words of Jesus as found in John 16:33 seem

appropriate right here. "In the world you will have tribulation. But take heart, I have overcome the world."

Acts 20:18–26

"You yourselves know how I lived among you the whole time from the first day that I set foot in Asia, serving the Lord with all humility and with tears and with trials that happened to me through the plots of the Jews, how I did not shrink from declaring to you anything that was profitable, and teaching you in public and from house to house, testifying both to Jews and to Greeks of repentance toward God and of faith in our Lord Jesus Christ. And now behold, I am going to Jerusalem, constrained by the Spirit, not knowing what will happen to me there, except that the Holy Spirit testifies to me in every city that imprisonment and afflictions await me. But I do not account my life of any value nor as precious to myself, if only I may finish my course and the ministry that I received from the Lord Jesus, to testify to the gospel of the grace of God. And now, behold, I know that none of you among whom I have gone about proclaiming the kingdom will see my face again. Therefore I testify to you this day that I am innocent of the blood of all of you, for I did not shrink from declaring to you the whole counsel of God.

As Paul's third missionary journey winds down, he intends to go to Jerusalem. While on his way, he is able to gather the elders of the Ephesian Church to meet with him at the port city of Miletus, so he might encourage this new church. He begins by describing his form of ministry among them. Part of his presentation is "how I did not shrink from declaring to you anything that was profitable, and teaching you in public and from house to house."

And just before Paul comes to the end of his address he says again, "I did not shrink from declaring to you the whole counsel of God."

These are the words of a bold preacher of the gospel message.

Acts 28:30-31

He lived there two whole years at his own expense, and welcomed all who came to him, proclaiming the kingdom of God and teaching about the Lord Jesus Christ with all boldness and without hindrance.

Luke concludes his account of how the gospel

spread, according to the statement of Jesus in Acts 1:8, to "the end of the earth," which likely meant Rome in that era and in the thinking of Luke.

Paul in the custody (chained) of a Roman soldier, "with all boldness" proclaimed the kingdom of God. This is how Acts ends. From the beginning of Luke's history of the early Church to his conclusion we find the word **bold.** It is completely evident that biblical Christianity is evangelical.

Nothing Has Changed

The early church, as we see in the Book of Acts— and which Paul's, Peter's, and John's letters plainly reveal—obeyed Jesus' commands. This mission is a large part of what it means to be a follower of Jesus.

Let it be clear: this is not all of what Christ's disciples are called to. Loving the neighbor, caring for the poor, whom we always have with us, and reaching out to others who are in distress and pain—is also what we are called to. The Church has done so throughout its history, and sometimes those who are helped in one way or the other will hear the gospel and become followers of Jesus. Yet many will make some sort of confession of faith or unite with those who reach out to them, not because they are genuinely converted by the power of the Holy Spirit, but because they are in need and will embrace whatever doctrines and observances the caregiver provides.

Paul speaks of his ministry to the Thessalonians in his first letter to that church. In chapter 2:1–8 he gives us a model of how Christians of all eras may conduct their evangelism. It is likely Paul grew into this as the years went on and as he experienced his missionary work. Perhaps he was like many of us are in the early years following our conversion. We were aggressive, even obnoxious, pushy, threatening (I cringe), arrogant, and less than loving. Thus, it is important that we grasp the following words from Paul:

> For you yourselves know, brothers, that our coming to you was not in vain. But though we had already suffered and been shamefully treated at Philippi, as you know, we had boldness in our God to declare to you the gospel of God in the midst of much conflict. For our appeal does not spring from error or impurity or any attempt to deceive, but just as we have been approved by God to be entrusted with the gospel, so we speak, not to please man, but to please God who tests our hearts. For we never came with words of flattery, as you know, nor with a pretext for greed—God is witness. Nor did we seek glory from people, whether from you or from others, though we could have made

demands as apostles of Christ. But we were gentle among you, like a nursing mother taking care of her own children. So, being affectionately desirous of you, we were ready to share with you not only the gospel of God but also our own selves, because you had become very dear to us.

The first three verses in Paul's letter to Titus speak of the commission he had received from "God our Savior." My experience tells me that Christians often miss the incredible implications found in them. At the conclusion of this chapter, let us look more carefully at these verses inspired by the Holy Spirit:

Paul, a servant of God and an apostle of Jesus Christ, for the sake of the faith of God's elect and their knowledge of the truth, which accords with godliness, in hope of eternal life, which God, who never lies, promised before the ages began and at the proper time manifested in his word through the preaching with which I have been entrusted by the command of God our Savior (Titus 1:1–3).

Paul, the servant, was one sent by Jesus Christ, so that the elect of God would come to both faith and the knowledge of the truth. And this was accomplished by God his Savior who entrusted him with preaching what was in accord with "his word." There is no greater work than to be commanded to preach Jesus, and all of his followers are called to this. Some bring the word to great audiences, some to very small audiences, but no matter. The sending is the great thing.

Chapter Three
Biblical Evangelicals

As previously noted in the preface, the term *evangelicals* has been politicized in the last few decades. Thus, biblically oriented evangelicals have been tarnished with the broad-brush stroke used by those who do not understand the terminology. Evangelicals, in the biblical sense, are dismissed as being a voting bloc. One of the reasons for this chapter is to correct this false impression.

What is an Evangelical?

Evangelicals, the term itself, describes those whose focus is the preaching of the message of the gospel. Faith in Jesus comes by means of the presentation of who Jesus is and what Jesus did. The Holy Spirit of God convicts us of our sin and reveals Jesus to us.

Conviction of sin is quite different from remorse. During my thirty-two years of ministering in San Quentin Prison, it was not uncommon to find those who were remorseful over the events that led to their incarceration. This is not repentance. Of course, anyone will feel terrible about losing his or her freedom and being locked up in a terrible place away from family and friends for long years.

Conviction of sin, when the Convictor is the Holy Spirit, is the certainty that one has offended a holy and righteous God, which must result in separation from Him for eternity.

Faith comes to us when we see that Jesus is our only hope of forgiveness and salvation. Jesus, who formerly meant little to us, now is revealed by the Holy Spirit to be our Savior. This, as Paul made so clear, is not the result of anything we do, or see, or learn, or anything else including wonderful good deeds. (See Ephesians 2:8-9 on this point.)

The preaching of the Gospel is offensive. Christian witnesses have often experienced that those who are offended and turn from Jesus often don't understand the reasons for their feelings. It is as Jesus said as recorded in Luke 23:34:

> "Father, forgive them, for they know not what they do."

This wonderful statement by Jesus concerning those who placed Him on the cross is the attitude of the evangelical. We see opposition as the understandable reaction of sinners confronted by a holy God. The convicting power of the Holy Spirit is often sharp and painful. Imagine the conflict: the word of grace engaged in mortal combat with the forces of hell.

The Messenger and the Message

Evangelicals must not take rejection personally. I have failed here many times; it is very human to react to what may seem to be personal rejection or assault.

The messenger is far easier to attack than the message. Jesus was the only pure evangelist, yet many found reason to reject Him, demean Him, brutalize Him, and put Him to death. Christians often admit that prior to their conversion they were the same—the convicted one will take out his or her frustration and confusion on the messenger—of course. The Christian witness might even be surprised to find people eager to hear the message.

The Adversary

There is an additional element at work, that is Satan, a name that means adversary or that "hideous strength," as C.S. Lewis put it. This defeated but powerful enemy hates Jesus and the gospel and will do everything to tarnish the preacher and the message preached. That there is a real spiritual warfare is without question. We do not fight against individuals so much as we struggle against a far greater opponent.

> For we do not wrestle against flesh and blood, but against the rulers, against the

authorities, against the cosmic powers over this present darkness, against the spiritual forces of evil in the heavenly places. (Ephesians 6:12)

Paul, in the passage above, speaks of putting on the whole armor of God, so that we may be able to stand firm against the assault of the enemy.

First, he presents the "belt of truth." This truth is Jesus—the way, the truth, and the life. It is not our truth, we have not made it up; it has been given to us.

Second comes the "breastplate of righteousness." We have no righteousness of our own, since we are sinners saved by grace. The evangelist must firmly grasp this.

Third, the feet of the readiness of the gospel of peace. We go out not to be troublemakers but agents of peace, and that peace is with God. Blessed indeed are the peacemakers.

Fourth, we carry in front of us the shield of faith. We do not trust ourselves, since we are not able to carry the fight alone. In our own strength and understanding, in our small ability and knowledge, we are weak.

Five, the helmet of salvation. We are not out saving ourselves, since we have been saved and that is that. This is security, this is strength. We go out onto the field having already won the battle.

Six, the sword of the Spirit, sharper than any two-edged sword. Our skill at debate and persuasion get us nowhere. But the written Word of God is powerful to tear down strongholds.

All of the above is accompanied by praying at all times that God would empower our witness and call those whom He will.

The Great Adventure

One thing I have noticed in my own life and in the lives of so many other followers of Jesus is that our lives are not boring as we engage in the greatest of adventures, that is, obeying the command of Jesus to preach the gospel to all the world.

Perhaps I have a greater need for challenges than most. While my prison work, baseball coaching, legal work as a process server and private detective, four-year military stint, street preaching in the Haight-Ashbury in the late 1960s, and a lot more, yet the most exciting part of my life is going on right now as a preacher of Jesus Christ and Him crucified. There is nothing like it, not even close.

Let me be clear. It is not all excitement; it is also an unusual kind of joy. I say "unusual," as I lack the ability to express this "joy unspeakable" any better.

Again let me say that the greatest of all adventures is to be a biblical evangelist. It is fulfilling in that it fills you with joy. Once you get a taste of it, once you put aside the fear of possible rejection and cease worrying about whether you can speak the right words but simply trust Him for results whether immediate or at some point in the future, you will be hooked on the great adventure. Excuse me if I use one more commonality: "It does not get any better."

Chapter Four

Presenting the Biblical Evangel

In the Book of Acts, we find the followers of Jesus showing up where groups of people gathered. These preachers followed the example of Jesus as we see Him in the Gospel accounts. And they ran into trouble as a result.

Stephen, the first martyr, preached in Jerusalem and encountered deadly opposition. Philip ranged far and wide, preaching as he went. Peter preached to a Gentile audience in Caesarea, and Paul, immediately following his conversion and throughout his ministry, presented Jesus the Messiah to Jews first and also to Gentiles.

Using a Biblical concordance, look up the words "bold" and "boldly." Luke uses these words to describe the preaching of Paul, Apollos, and others. The world in which they lived demanded boldness just as much as our world does today.

Digital Technology

Today, we have more opportunity for a bold witness

than any generation before us. At the recent National Religious Broadcasters Convention in Nashville—Proclaim18—there gathered a staggering array of means to present Jesus via television, radio, podcasting, film, and various streaming platforms, besides standard book publishing, with eBook and audio formats. Many of these digital formats reach around the world and into every nook and corner. It is simply amazing.

We are no longer, nor have we ever been, bound by walls. The entire world is reachable.

Over the last five years, congregants of Miller Avenue Baptist Church, with help from other church friends, have developed many of the above platforms to present dozens, even hundreds, of videos that have been viewed by thousands. Just this one simple process of filming, editing, and uploading videos is available to most of us, and it is not as difficult to accomplish as it used to be! If a non-techy person like me can do it, anyone can.

Let me express a caveat here: with so many avenues to pursue via the internet, the tendency can be to let new technology bypass the inter-personal proclaiming of Jesus' person and work. However, the local church is now, has been, and always will be the center of discipleship and evangelism. Other forms of evangelical presentation should result in some form of fellowship, direct and personal.

The Biblical Example

It has required a third time preaching through the Book of Acts for me to realize that the early apostles, missionaries, and evangelists did not employ any mechanism or methodology besides direct proclamation of the essential message of Jesus Christ and Him crucified. As Paul put it:

> And I, when I came to you, brothers, did not come proclaiming to you the testimony of God with lofty speech or wisdom. For I decided to know nothing among you except Jesus Christ and him crucified. And I was with you in weakness and in fear and much trembling, and my speech and my message were not in plausible words of wisdom, but in demonstration of the Spirit and of power, that your faith might not rest in the wisdom of men but in the power of God. (1 Corinthians 2:1–5)

I cannot say that I have always followed Paul's program. In the past, I employed various methodologies to draw people in. This I learned from seminary classes and from the Church Growth Seminars at Fuller Theological Seminary in Pasadena, CA, during the late 1980s.

Music became a focus and it worked, or so it seemed. I tried different group activities and practiced what might be called "relational evangelism," and this also seemed to work. Then the church I pastored tried meeting the needs of others in terms of free food. And to a small degree, this seemed effective as well.

One technique I did not do, though I learned it from John Wimber while at Fuller, was to emphasize signs and wonders, especially healing. Nor did I attempt to create a wild and ecstatic type of worship service. Actually, I was just not able to pull that one off, which is just as well, since those who engage in some of the practices stated above tend to produce temporary results and sadly, false conversions. We find that if people feel blessed and happy they will keep coming. However, that wears thin after a while. Frankly, efforts to keep up the excitement become a burden.

How It Works

"So faith comes from hearing, and hearing through the word of Christ" (Romans 10:17), is a passage painted on the wall facing the preacher when standing at the pulpit at Miller Avenue Baptist Church.

Paul captured the core of it. The preacher proclaims who Jesus is and what Jesus did. The Holy Spirit then convicts of sin and judgment and points to Jesus and

His dying on the cross and His resurrection from the dead. Only the Holy Spirit can do this. The witness, preacher, or evangelist cannot do this. We depend upon the inner working of the Holy Spirit.

A clever manipulative person might be able to get people out of the pew, or get hands raised, or give out a prayer to be prayed. In the 1970s, I did so hundreds of times and saw hundreds or more seemingly make commitments. I was good at it.

For a time, I was invited to many summer camps for kids in the junior and high school age bracket. It was simple to get every single kid up front and on their knees. Yes, I did so, and sometimes without ever even speaking an actual gospel message. A good story told with passion was often enough. I am embarrassed to recall this now, and it may be one of the reasons that prompted this little book.

The witness is not responsible for anything except to explain the story of Jesus. Then the Holy Spirit goes to work to convince of sin and reveal Jesus. Like in the Parable of the Sower, the word is sown, presented in whatever manner, and that is that.

What a relief it is to the preacher to understand this!

A Reality the Evangelical Must Understand

Paul, in the second chapter of 2 Corinthians, speaks of two different ways in which the message of the gospel is experienced:

> For we are the aroma of Christ to God among those who are being saved and among those who are perishing, to one a fragrance from death to death, to the other a fragrance from life to life. Who is sufficient for these things? (2 Corinthians 2:15–16)

It is wonderful to see people come to faith in Christ; a person estranged from God is now born anew. This is the "fragrance" from life to life. Then there is the stench of death which will be experienced by the evangelist as well. No one likes the smell, especially the one mired in death, and this lost person may react, sometimes violently, against the messenger, the one thought to be responsible for the very ugly fragrance. Previous to his conversion, Paul (then known as Saul) had a murderous reaction to the followers of Jesus.

As one reads through the life of Jesus in the Gospels we see many who hated and abused Him, finally to the point of death. As one reads through the Book of Acts we see the same for evangelists like Stephen,

James the Apostle, and Paul. It is said, likely with considerable accuracy, that all the apostles except John died a martyr's death. Then throughout the history of the Church we discover many persecutions which extend to this day. It might be that in our own day this murderous persecution is picking up steam.

Yes, the fragrance from death to death should be expected by the witness for Jesus. We know that, as Christians, we may be publicly rewarded for good deeds done for those in need, but we also know that the world does not like to be challenged by exposing sin and warning of judgment.

Counting the cost of obeying the call to preach the gospel to the entire world is necessary. When we do so, we will be encouraged by James 1:2: "Count it all joy, my brothers, when you meet trials of various kinds, for you know that the testing or your faith produces steadfastness."

Chapter Five

The Alternative

Meeting Needs

The prime alternative to the bold proclamation of Jesus for many Christians, churches, and whole denominations is to aim at meeting felt needs. Indeed, many in the evangelical tradition engage in these forms of authentic ministry. But this good work is not the same as the straight forward presentation of the core gospel message. The question is: May both function simultaneously?

The following are views of the Christian mission that fall short of the biblical agenda:

- God rewards those who faithfully practice their religion.

- God will show favor to those who minister to the physical needs of others.

- God wants us to focus on saving the enviroment.

- God wants us to participate in the political process for the freedom of the oppressed.

- God calls us to help the poor so that they will be saved.

The list could be far longer, and Scripture endorses all of the above to one degree or another. Yet none of these is able to secure the only thing that really matters and that is eternal life in the presence of God.

Christians may be rewarded in the here and now for engaging in social and political actions which are approved by the local culture, even garnering news coverage and honors. It has happened to me, particularly regarding volunteering to engage with convicts in prison. This does not negate the possible favorable impact of the work of Christians who reach out to those in need, but however wonderful and magnanimous the outreach may be, it is not a substitute for gospel preaching.

Some say, "Do both," and perhaps this is possible, but I have rarely experienced a truly integrated combination with both gospel proclamation power and sustained altruistic action. It is usually one approach or the other.

Another issue is that reaching out to those in need receives a welcoming and seemingly grateful audience, but it is often disingenuous. Those who are in need may be accommodating to those who provide services and may speak well of them but ignore the message, because people in need tend to affirm whatever the caregiver presents.

For some twenty-five years Miller Avenue Baptist Church has conducted a food giveaway program, and we are careful not to take advantage of this situation by pressing those who benefit to attend services. While everyone is welcome, the desire and/or need to please a benefactor may be an improper motivation, and false or temporary "conversions" often result.

During the hippie movement in San Francisco, I lived in a rescue mission in the City's Fillmore District. Every evening a crowd of young, mostly white hip types walked in the door at dinnertime. Before they could eat they had to listen to me preach.

Now, during the day I walked and preached on the streets of the Haight-Ashbury District and saw many come to faith in Christ by means of a simple presentation of the person and work of Jesus. I had nothing to offer anyone except Jesus.

This is not to say that a church or group of Christians ought not to reach out to those in need. But this should not be considered evangelism. Gospel preaching and helping those in need are two different things.

Preaching a Works-Based Religion

There are essentially two kinds of religion. The first

emphasizes performing rites and rituals, accepting the religion's worldview, and adopting the religion's identity as a true believer.

The most vivid example of this is Islam. It is works based, where the only sure means of ending up in Paradise is to die in violent jihad with a Muhammad-like smile on one's face.

Hinduism, to offer a second example, teaches that over the course of many re-incarnations one might reach enlightenment. In Western countries certain gurus have lightened the load by teaching that unity with the godhead may be achieved in a single incarnation.

Amazingly, this same message may be heard in mainstream Christianity. Without actually stating it, the impression is given that a person is able to achieve a right relationship with God through right belief and good works. This message is attractive. The message that we are to turn from sin and trust Jesus as Savior and Lord—the core gospel message—is offensive and off-putting.

During the late 1980s to the mid 1990s, we at Miller Avenue discovered we could grow the congregation by a combination of strategies: meeting felt needs, providing good entertainment by means of a band, preaching shorter sermons, providing free food after the service, involving people in outreach programs, and above all, not preaching anything at all about sin, judgment, and hell. It worked for a time. But typically, people would move on to a venue that was more exciting and entertaining, especially if that group that made them feel good about themselves.

In the broad spectrum of Christianity is found many who merely teach that doing certain things or believing certain things is the way to salvation and eternal life in heaven. Be baptized, become a member of the church, sign on to the church's statement of faith, observe the prescribed rituals and rites, e.g., receive the sacraments on a regular basis, and one's place in heaven is thereby secured. These are all undertakings that depend on the authority and power of the particular church involved rather than the person's individual relationship with God through Jesus Christ. This is works-based religion, not Bible-based faith.

Authentic, biblical Christianity preaches that salvation is a gift that cannot be earned. Faith in Jesus as Savior is a gift, which no one can attain on his or her own. Apart from the working of the Holy Spirit, no one, however good, will be saved.

The entire process of coming to faith in Jesus is a work of God. The Holy Spirit reveals to us our great need, because our breaking of God's law means we are condemned and guilty. The Holy Spirit reveals to us the Savior, Jesus Christ the righteous One, who has taken all our sin upon Himself on the cross. Buried, He carried our sin away—every bit, past, present, and future. He rose from the dead, is alive forevermore, and gives us the gift of eternal life as a result. This is the ultimate intention of the Creator God.

Moreover, this gift comes to us through the preaching—the simple proclamation—of Jesus Christ. As Paul wrote in Romans 10:17: "So faith comes from hearing, and hearing through the word of Christ."

The alternative of preaching a works-based religion, whether in a Christian/biblical context or not, leads to ultimate deception and error.

Chapter Six
Anti-Evangelism

It is not expected that every sermon and every emphasis from Christian pulpits should be of an evangelistic nature. As a pastor, I realize the need for presentations on numbers of important topics that are not directly evangelical in nature. However, there are some subjects, issues, and concepts that I consider to be anti-evangelistic. I am likely to offend some now, but please hear me out.

Is Science the Enemy?

- Must a seeker after truth and salvation reject science and take Genesis chapters one to eleven literally?

- Is it possible to have saving faith in Jesus and not believe in a literal six-day creation scenario?

- Is a person hopeless if they reject a worldwide flood during the days of Noah?

- Does affirming "Intelligent Design" fall short of the biblical mark?

- What if a person thinks the universe was created out of nothing (ex-nihilo) thirteen billion and not five thousand years ago?

As Christians we are free to choose and adopt views on many subjects, although the Bible is silent on many issues and leaves the disciple to discern his or her own way. And although a high percentage of us have arrived at very close to the same positions, having "right" views never saved anyone.

When I was first converted, I was tantamount to a total pagan and endorsed UFOs, Edgar Cayce, and other crazy ideas. I clung to these with great energy, yet one by one they fell away. Most of us are similar, in that we came to faith with a garbage bag full of ideas gathered from the culture around us. A disciple is just that—a disciple—a learner in the ways of the Lord. Over the course of my ministry I have enjoyed watching God grow people up into more of the fullness of Christ.

Must a Person Be Sin-free?

- "Clean up your act!" You can't be a Christian if you . . .

- "Repentance, without which you cannot be saved, means you must turn from all your sin."

Well into the Christian life, I am still busy repenting of my sin. If I had been aware of all my sin at the time of my conversion by the Holy Spirit, I would have been overwhelmed with grief. In fact, as Christians grow into our sanctification we become even more grieved about our sinful ways, sometimes to the point of deep inner pain. And in case we thought we would ever get past them, we are often reminded of the stupid and sinful ways in which we have continued while being followers of Jesus. These are even more difficult to deal with. Hardly a day goes by that Christians do not commit sin, even if it is only in our thoughts.

The focus of repentance is more about changing the mind as to who Jesus is than putting away sin. It is growing up in Christ that sin begins to fade away. The primary word usually translated "repent" in the Greek New Testament means to change the mind, and the change is in how we view Jesus. Prior to conversion He might have been little more than a swear word, but then we changed.

I am not saying that we *may* continue in sin. Not at all; we are called to turn away from sin. As time goes on we discover more and more about what is not pleasing to our heavenly Father. Yet, we sin, some are led astray, rebel even, but we do not lose our salvation as a result. It is a long growing up into Christ and no one will achieve sinless perfection. We have "no license to sin," and sin becomes distasteful and horrid in the process of following Jesus.

Must One Have the Proper View on Social, Moral, and Political Issues?

Abortion, politics, immigration, same-sex marriage, political identity, gun control, etc., may be critical issues, and there may be right and wrong positions to hold, biblically speaking, but having the correct views is meaningless when it comes to Holy Spirit conversion. Some think they are genuine Christians simply because they are against the "wrong" views or are for the "right" views on social, moral, and political issues.

Regarding homosexuality, Christians regard the homosexual act to be unbiblical and ultimately harmful for the individual, both now and in eternity (see 1 Corinthians 6:9–10). Regarding abortion, many consider it outright murder and think that unless one is absolutely opposed to it, he or she is nothing more than a baby killer.

Far left or far right political positions act as a barrier. Christians will have strong feelings about politics, but when the gospel is presented alongside a political point of view, the mark is missed. We must care more about reaching people for Christ than promoting a political agenda, no matter how vital and correct that agenda appears to be. We must rely on the Holy Spirit, through the lifelong process of discipleship, to turn hearts and minds to the things of God.

54

Counterfeit Spiritual Experiences

There is presently a very strong emphasis within a growing segment of the church on having a direct experience with divine spiritual entities. I recently spoke with a person who hears regularly from an archangel as well as a spirit animal. These direct personal encounters can be strong convincers that one has a saving relationship with God.

Faith, in the biblical sense, seems vacant and disappointing to many, especially those who are merely Christianized. The need to be assured of salvation for those who have only experienced false conversion may well create a desire to seek confirmation through a direct experience with God.

Those needs and desires have fueled aspects of worship in some charismatic/Pentecostal settings where emphasis is now on direct contact with the supernatural. Moving and grooving to the beat of a drum and bass guitar during a wild and exuberant "worship" time can produce a state of mind not unlike that found in shamanistic expressions such as Santería and Wicca and in other religious and non-religious forms that emphasize the ecstatic experience.

Such experiences are real and very spiritual but have nothing to do with biblical Christianity; they are, in fact, a demonic deception. Consider the words of Jesus from Matthew 24:24: "For false Christs and false prophets will arise and perform great signs and wonders, so as to lead astray, if possible, even the elect." Then, from the Sermon on the Mount we find Jesus teaching,

> "Not everyone who says to me, 'Lord, Lord,' will enter the kingdom of heaven, but the one who does the will of my Father who is in heaven. On that day many will say to me, 'Lord, Lord, did we not prophesy in your name and cast out demons in your name, and do many mighty works in your name? And then will I declare to them, 'I never knew you; depart from me, you workers of lawlessness.'" Matthew 7:21-23

Despite what the new apostles and prophets are saying, our Christian faith and our Scripture is not temporary; we are not "off the charts," and God is not "doing something new" in the sense of jettisoning the Bible. Therefore, we do not seek God outside biblical norms. We reject the notion that we do not need the Word which has supposedly been superseded by the words of the apostles and prophets designated for "these final days." We reject the idea that we are becoming gods.

Though attractive, tempting, and crowd pleasing,

this is not the focus of biblical Christianity.

Reporting Numbers of Conversions

When I gained the reputation of counting many conversions at youth camps, I honed my skills and heightened that status. My invitations were so emotionally compelling that few could resist either coming forward or raising a hand, and this by the hundreds.

Were all these true conversions to Christ? With the retrospect of decades now of evaluating my evangelistic tactics, I have come to see that some, hopefully not too many, were falsely converted. Salvation is all of God through the working of the Holy Spirit to convict of sin and reveal Jesus as the Savior. Salvation is not an emotional experience, though emotion may be involved.

The work of the evangelist is to present the Person and Work of Jesus Christ, the Word become flesh who, on the cross paid the awful price for our sin. This is the work—this alone.

Going Directly to the Work

Our focus must be on the large issues of life and death. We all die biologically, but we all live on forever—there is the resurrection to heaven and to hell.

Jesus said,

> "Do not marvel at this, for an hour is coming when all who are in the tombs will hear his voice, and come out, those who have done good to the resurrection of life, and those who have done evil to the resurrection of judgment." (John 5:28-29; see also Daniel 12:2)

Chapter Seven

Biblical Christianity is Evangelical

Lastly is a summary of the primary thesis of this book: Christians are called to be proclaimers of the simple gospel message, trusting in the Holy Spirit to do the work of conversion. All else, however important, is secondary.

Preaching through the Book of Acts a third time reminded me once again that the followers of Jesus were focused on fulfilling the great commission. I highly recommend Michael Green's book, *Evangelism in the Early Church*, which clearly shows the evangelical nature of those believers.

Christian unity can be found in the evangelic mission. Of the 45,000 plus denominations that have arisen since the Reformation, there is little unity in terms of authority, doctrine, worship style, and organization. My contention is that true unity among Christians worldwide, regardless of organizational identity, is to be found in a shared evangelical passion.

Yes, at the core of biblical Christianity is unity for all Christians of whatever name is written above the door through which they walk. The straightforward message of grace in and through the cross of Jesus Christ unifies us all. Those who say salvation is only through *our* group operate under the influence of a cultic mindset.

Christians from all over the world at conventions like the NRB (National Religious Broadcasters) and the Christian Booksellers Association's ICRS (International Christian Retailer's Show) demonstrate that there is a unity at the core—spreading the gospel message. Few if any of us attending such conferences ever bother to ask about another person's organizational identity. We know right away we have fellowship and connection in Christ. My decades of authoring books and meeting with other Christian authors have proven that Christians from unexpected groups have found value in work that is completely mainline evangelical—evangelical in the commonly understood definition. Let us not judge outward appearances carelessly.

Meeting with Coptic Christians from the Middle East, Greek and Russian Orthodox priests, Roman Catholics from all over, Anglicans, Seventh Day Adventists, and many others, has confirmed that, despite some rather strong doctrinal differences, Christians of many stripes share the work of presenting Jesus to a lost and dying world. Rather than belaboring this point, let us conclude that the unity of the world-wide Body of Christ, that Church known only to our Triune God, is seen in biblically oriented evangelism.

One Last Word

In the grand and wonderful story of "Jesus and the Woman of Samaria" (John 4:1-45) is a most wonderful saying of Jesus. The single sentence statement by Jesus may be why this singular and rather lengthy story is even found in the Bible. Here is my summary of the passage:

Stopping at a well while travelling through a virtual no-man's land in Samaria, Jesus' disciples go into a neighboring town for supplies. Meanwhile, Jesus, alone at the well, begins to speak to a Samaritan woman who had come to draw water.

This woman right away recognizes the unorthodox nature of the encounter; a Jewish man simply would not normally speak to a Samaritan woman whose religious views were counter to those of a Galilean Jew. Despite cultural conventions, Jesus initiates a conversation with the Samaritan woman.

It does not take long before the woman realizes there is something special about Jesus, who tells her about her life experiences in the past. She rushes back into the city from which she came stating to her town's folks, "Come, see a man who told me all that I ever did."

Jesus' disciples return, shocked to find Him speaking with such a person, but they choose not to say a word. Their only concern is that Jesus should eat something. Then Jesus says,

> "I have food to eat that you do not know about."

This is the wonderful saying of Jesus. And it is for us as well, for us who boldly proclaim the gospel message. This is what drives us on the greatest of all adventures. We never get enough of it.

There is a bit more to the story. The disciples urge Jesus to eat. They wonder if someone else brought Him food. Jesus' reply is,

> "My food is to do the will of him who sent me, and to accomplish his work."

And have we not also been sent?

> "As the Father has sent me, even so I am sending you." (John 20:21)

A Prayer of the Anglican Church of West Malaysia

Almighty God, we thank you for having renewed your church, at various times and in various ways, by rekindling the fire of love for you through the work of your Holy Spirit. Rekindle your love to our hearts and renew us to fulfill the Great Commission which your Son committed to us; so that, individually and collectively, as members of your Church we may help many to know Jesus Christ as their Lord and Saviour. Empower us by your Spirit to share, with our neighbours and friends, our human stories in the context of your divine story; through Jesus Christ our Lord. Amen

Invitation and Challenge

If you want to know whether Jesus is who He said He is and if Jesus is what the Bible says He is and if what historical Christianity also says He is, here is an invitation and a challenge.

It is a challenge, because when you find out that Jesus is real, it will change your life, and not just a little.

At a time when you really want to know if Jesus is real, simply ask Him: "Jesus are you real? If you are, let me know it."

It is impossible to describe how the answer might come to you. Over the centuries there have been hundreds of differing ways Jesus answers. But you will know.

Warning: the path of following Jesus is narrow, and it is likely in this present culture that many will not be pleased with you becoming a Christian. Authentic Christians will be persecuted. You must count the cost.

If an answer does not come quickly, do not give up. Keep asking.

www.ingramcontent.com/pod-product-compliance
Lightning Source LLC
Chambersburg PA
CBHW060713030426
42337CB00017B/2852